Flights of Emotions

My Life is an Airport

Author Katenna Adderley

Dedication

To my Lord and Savior Jesus Christ with a faith of a mustard seed he has always provided for me and my family.

My love my heart begins and ends. The women to breathe life in me my mother Yvonne Adderley and Great grandmother Loretta T. Jones. Rest In Heaven

My Aunt M and Aunt E my new mothers that has been on me with hugs, love, and sometimes ropes.

My sisters the one that are real and the ones I've adopted. I love you. Thank you for your support. Quick Shout out Coco, Nina, Kesha, Tanya, Arlisha, Jamesha, Jante, Elisha, Silvia, and Shariece.

My brothers all real Samuel and Arlize who has really been more like fathers to me.

The three men in my life that I love above and beyond the heavens and stars.

And to the Selling Katenna fam with your support my dream is becoming my reality with all my love.

Contents

Intermit Proportions 7
The Devil in Me 7
The Passion for Fruit 9
Jealousy 9
(Corrupt) Infatuation 10
Politic 11
My Journey at Sea 11
To Love 12
Lover 13
Drowning 14
Mirrors 15
Sleep 16
My Existence (ME) 17
Needless Thing 18
Great 19
Forward 19
Some Things 20
Spare Me 21
Why vs. How 22
The Words for Sin 24
My Word 25
The Memo 26
I Am 27
I'm Selling Myself 29
Pity Party 30
Hurt 31
I Love That Nigger 32
The Essence of Kay 33
You Don't Know 34
Him 35
That 36
Time 37
My Mr. Gray 38
The Lady 40
Her 41

Super Hero	42
Ebony Queen	43
My Rose (LTJ)	44
Sister of Me	44
Mother Love	45
Irrational	46
(I Am) The She in Me	47
With These Words	48
Letter to Myself	48
Fallen (Wasted)	49
Passing By	50
A Broken Love Song	51
The Love I Want	52
Sold	53
Twin	55
Could I Kill	56
Final Words	57

Baring my soul to the world.

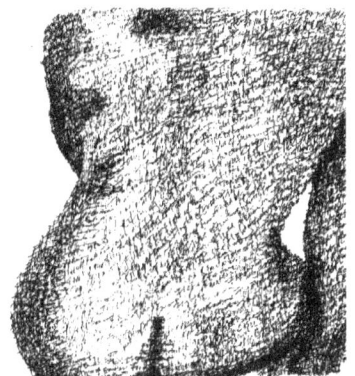

Intermit Proportions

I touch the light, so smooth, so soft it teases me with its heat. It's there you know, there where virgins go to lose the eternity of paradise. So ripe for the taste the moisture stains your wet lip with the juice of its seed. As I watch the flesh leave the corpus of his soul to fill the night with his hunger. I scream but the words are clot at the eternal level of silence it comes out as a soft breeze of whispers. Any journey of hell could not be more pleasurable than the heaven of stretching the levee of Eve's bosoms. A cry so sweet the depth of its fever explodes in a zenith of ones' heat bursting with stars of light. A call so strong, so dark, the strength of gratifying passion brings a hurricane thrust of endless delightful ache. Forcing the earth among the crest edges of the world, but no man will ever live up to the raff of the almighty God Zeus serpent. What can I say, vanity in it's oldest form could not perish the heart of one so vain to the desire of beauty. It is the great perfection of movement with the continuous flow of organic milky white explosions. It is at the heart of my soul.

The Devil in Me

The devil made me do it I cannot tell a lie.
Enticing me from the great kingdom in the sky
Charming me to his heated retreat
With a promise of a heavenly delightful treat.
He led me though hell on a powerful horse
And when I realize my mistake he shows no remorse,
Pulling me back when I tried to run
Torching my soul with the burning sun.
The devil made me do it I cannot tell a lie.

Hear the angels in heaven's deafening cries.
Carrying me to his lair intensify in flame
Tears from heaven with whispers of his name
Laying me on his enormous bed blaze with fire
Groaning his exotic dreams and most intimate desire
As the heat incinerates my clothes to dust
His body consumes with razor-sharp lust.

The devil made me do it I cannot tell a lie.
Plunging in my body making me fly
Holding me down as he was driven insane
Consuming him whole with a syrupy sweetness of pain,
Giving off the heated fire of his torch soul
Puree of liquid metal more fine than gold
With his wicked pleasure dominating every cell
He tormented my soul and dared me to tell.

The devil made me do it I cannot tell a lie.
Taking me above heaven to a place so high
A beast among demons he continued his thrust
With in an explosion of power my body was crushed.
Never relenting on his fixation-craved assault
Worshiping my ruination with praises in a cult.
He wanted it all, my heart, spirit, body and soul
With me under him he wanted ultimate control.

The devil made me do it I cannot tell a lie.
Taking over my core I thought I would die
As the passion slipped from spirit, my mind became cold
Chaining my body as he seized my soul.
I was lost in his world adrift in a sea
It wasn't the beast that made me do it; it was the devil in me.

The Passion for Fruit

I taste the purity of its juice as it drops in my mouth, the smooth juicy overspill slips down my lips. I lick the wet flavor from my fingers, the rich sweetness flows over the pallet of my tongue. Its makes me hunger
The temptress of liquid that teases me with the naked heat of its taste I want it, I need it, I must have it. Like the addicted pursuing the ultimate drug. I'm waiting for the moment of fulfilling the sweet desire of my most intermit craving. The passion of fruit

Jealousy

It's under the bed. A dangerous beast with evil at the core of its existence; I feel it watching me. Its eyes are flaming red with angry demons spoiling for release. Demons that used the minds' rebellion and deception to draw a bleed of pain from the soul. It's waiting for me in the dark with no shadow to show its movements. He calls but I do not answer. For I know the call is to trap me within my own fears. I dare not close my eyes for he shall know and overtake me. I dare not think of sleep to do so will only make me weak. Oh if he could leave me alone only then am I able to survive. He keeps coming back as if I don't know he's deadly. When I see him he is the center of life, the sun in which the planets orbit around leveling the essence of me in my true form. However if one shall ever touch the sun the burn will consume you to ash. He is everything we adore and everything we detest. The beast is something that can stand alone but will bring down massively in its wake.

He is his own enemy. For then if he shall ever become me I shall dissolve in destruction.

(Corrupt) Infatuation

The promise of your touch is not nearly enough but yet the pleasure is so sweet I savor it. I wish to be…
Swear unto me all my hearts' desire. Lay what you refuse to give me at my feet, and I shall give you undying devotion. Stop telling me lies unless the lie shall be the words I craved to hear. I wish to… be….
Perish the thought that I shall be forever under your spell perhaps then I will breathe and exist once more. Heed, that I alone am destined for torture and that the wickedness of a man shall be my damnation in hell. And what shall they say after my demise: "hah! Hah! Hah! A foolish one so young and forgotten." I wish to be…I wish…
Oh but I go so willingly that it sickens my soul. I am the unbigoted lamb going to slaughter, poor me that when I am in your midst I became your whore. With the scent of seduction in the air to seep into our pores, and your absolute passion of nature is to empower yourself with strength. Begging for your stroke and only relenting to your bliss of contentment. I wish… Oh I wish… I wish to be…
Did you forget what lay behind closed doors? Can you not see that I have sacrificed what is now lost in time? Am I deceiving the identity of what remains that I have become? Fuck to be and fuck not to be. Because I wish… to be… I wish to be…. Loved…

Politic

The darkness consumes me. The black inky poison slips up the body with the mind to control. All that is will dissolve as it pours the essence of loathing in its wake. Trying to consume alive or dead everything in its path. Drops of madness form the wicked ways of man carrying the burden of life to the ultimate ending. The taste of fear manipulates what you may see as ruthless. Like the mighty lion he is a king walking among our planet and we are the weak-minded servants. What can I say about a man who paints pictures of paradise with the point of his finger? Who whisper hate as he thrusts his steel into your drenched cave of tender flesh. Whose broken promises are his way of existence? Whose lies give birth to worlds? What we see is only the beginning as more and more we relive birth, life, and death. He will not stop until life has taken the last of him. Know your mind, standing for something and not believing is much worse then falling for everything.

My Journey at Sea

Push the calls
Take the calls
Break the calls
Make the call
I arrived on board the ship happy and glee
Knowing I could have raisin in time at three
My mouth was dirty more than the sailor
Lying in bed were me and my jailor
The captain has lost his arm his leg
With a person to talk not plead or beg
With debt to the old and pain to young

With a chord around my heart my mind was hung.
I watch the infamous Moby chase the Dick
But the whale lies move was much too quick
With the wind at my shoulder and the water at my hand
Before I walk the plank I had a master plan
It was here I thought I had won the game
But an animal nature is never the same
It would plot and connive to save its skin
Even plan a decoy that comes as a friend
The stage was set I had my final call
How proud she was that I would take the fall
In deep water I almost drown
Then I came up for air weighing pound for pound
I was alive and living so well
I am the only one who survived to tell
As the story goes on the whale got away
But she will always remember me on that day
Push the calls
Take the calls
Break the calls
Make the call

To Love

I'm in love. A love so smooth glistens like the diamond in its purest form. The old once upon a time prince, he is not. Slaying dragons breathing fire are long forgotten while he destroys the evil debt of my financial inaccuracies. My hero is a male who seeks justice with his pen and builds worlds with his dialect. Funny I'm most happy when he is passionately placing words on the chessboard of life a mastermind in his fineness. As the corny words of my youth play in my head "I love you more than I can say. My love is the sweet rain on a hot day giving the earth relief

from the drought. The liquid slit to moisten the land which only brings us together hand and hand." I am in love with a man that stands alone surrounded by thousands. He cannot be more perfect for me as he explains that only reason God formed Adam and Eve was because he knew that one day you and I would meet. That day all things would cease to be no more then a backdrop for our love. Like the stars surrounded by the moon there would be many stars but only one moon. I am in love. It's funny how the smile on my face is never gone and that his present is never far from my mind. I always used to say that love was just a mind game to get hooked on someone else's dreams. Now I say it is reality building two people together and binding them for a lifetime. I just want to jump off the highest mountain because the highest building would be too low to scream my words of love for him. I'm in love.
But no matter what anyone says the gift of love is the one thing in life we all seek. Some want it so bad that they can't breathe within it. Others fight it until it almost kills them to live without it. Then there are those that unconsciously want it to gravitate to love.
I just say love because it is the only thing in this life that could ever give us harmony.
I'm in love. He's in love. We're in love, to love…

Lover

How can I describe a god among men, who has pounded the very cord of my existence into diamonds of pleasure?
Do I said that the whisper of his name gives me chills that I transform in an orgasmic rush of heat?
That his touch scorches my being and every cell is incinerated from even the slightest blow of air from his breath.

And when he looks at me my body craves his sexual assault violating my mind to a forbidden hunger of bliss.
That the pursuit of lust leaves me wanting to be everything and anything his mind can conceive.
Just looking at the image of a god, which is just a shadow of the beast.
He is the dream of pleasure and passion, intertwined with the very soul I have surrendered to it master.
I am happy to bow to his perfection just to know he is a man which binds him to earth.
The forbidden fruit the plunge my mind into sins of deception.
Tilting the very world I exist into dreams of a beautiful utopia.
That the moan of his name equals pure sin as my body explodes in heaves which plummet my emotions into hell.
The only man I wish to touch the membrane of my flesh and contaminate my heart with his infected philosophy.
This man who has all power over my being that I am charged with imprisonment of his heart.
Without him this life does not exist, living is not an option and this is he who I call lover.

Drowning

It's where shallow waters become deep. I never knew how to swim but yet I drove in subconsciously. The water was to my liking and I wonder what would become of me if I should perish within these hours, between these minutes, among these seconds. I float as the abundance of water pours over my soul. Clear, cool, and calm in all the world there is no greater place. My mind wonders what I have now become. The youth of my days have now stilled with flow. I am listening to silence. I hear the words of a falling soldier as he draws his last breath on earth to go into the unknown, and it becomes clear, "I feel pain, I taste love, I touch life, I smell death, and I see peace. Time is not my enemy, life is." The fall when it comes takes you instantly, it is what life doesn't teach you that makes the difference. Don't panic it's said. Just stay calm but went your mind relive the life you led as a silence commerce for help. You fight. The struggle to come up for air is too great but this will only make you weak. The energy you used will dwindle to nothing. As your greatest fear pulls you down to meet the bottom. You scream, it's too much to hold on to as you slip into a blurry vision of survival. You cannot think your body unaware you have come to the surface again. You are unaware of your surrounds and only the quietness of your subconscious takes you with the stream. You go down in peace. Your eternity has ended and your dreams have stopped being still this lifetime.

Mirrors

I not a lesbian nor have I ever been with a woman. I state these facts only to say that many things inspire me. I am controlled by my writing and ruled by my thoughts. I cannot help that my emotions are brought on by the pleasures of others existent in my sphere. With this confession I shall explain further, a friend whispers in my ear of a secret meeting between himself and an anonymous woman. As his lips touch my ear arousing my soul my mind conjured up the scene. A simple person that has a simple life and spoke of a simple story made the bond of marriage her family, friend, and world. She is not beautiful he says but the sensual nature of her essence made him hunger to process the untutored novice. It did not take long for him to explain that she had come to his home bearing

gifts of freedom, salvation, and liberation through intercourse. He touched her, kissing her all over and I began to feel the butterfly tingle of needles on my fetish. Allowing her strokes across his craving body he was bestowing his natural perception for toleration of her need to be in control. As he goes on my mind absorbs every enchanted detail as his fingers find themselves between my thighs touching heated skin. He keeps taking me there spinning his tale to paradise with his touch and my deceiving imagination. I became him I feel her as she explored his body licking his skin feeling her way all over me. She looks at me with the fever of serenity, my soul is where she is trying to go. The smell of sweat burns my nose and consumes my brain cells until I call her by name. He does not stop, she does not stop I am in their mist I breathe through him trying to get to her. The reality keep me in suspense the image keeps me under the magician spell. He pushes me down I am above her our skins have touched I can feel her heartbeat see the light of perfection that is in her eyes. I can taste her kisses and feel
her nails plunge through my core. As my legs release and I felt the weight of his thighs with her hands all over me I become astray. He has gained complete domination over my being she thought, and she will not relent. He had me in her grip and just before I drown in a world beyond my knowledge he spoke "As I finally took her, she whispered to me 'The reason I chose you, is because… you're just like her'."

Sleep

I watch and wait for the bliss of love
A hope to feel affection from one so dangerous,
Like mating with the son of Lucifer,

Walking the road of damnation paved in gold trimmed in rubies,
I am my mother's child with a little of my father for a twist.
He is everything I want but nothing I need.
The force of his call keeps me wanting the man but also the forgotten beast.
Then I dream of him he who has given me a crystal heart.
The poison of my pain,
The hero of destruction whose seeds I contain.
I see him on a beast so wild with great speed.
It is he whose tears are my downfall, a virgin sacrifice that burns black in a flow of red.
I cannot stop my dreams, I block my thoughts I freeze my body, I am silent to words.
I lay in fear of sleep.
Again I want to taste, touch, and feel only him.
Taste the essence on the pallet of my tongue.
Awake. Blissful light oh to the heavens of opening my eyes and seeing the sun.

My Existence (ME)

How many times do I kill myself?
I feel foolish again, why do I set myself up every time
I hope things turn out for the best then I let myself down why is it that I keep thinking that this time would be different but it's not.
I can't help myself I fall so fast from so high in so deep.
I am labelled reckless.
Can't I just sleep the sleep of death?
Can't I just dream the dream that never ends?
Why do I do this to myself and live for regret.
I keep waiting for that moment in time when everything's still and happy. That place where everything is always

perfect and nothing matters. It is the palace of heaven where everyone walks around in bliss and their halo up with perfection.
Then the truth hit and I am the angel falling from the heaven damned for hell.
I can't stop myself.

Needless Thing

I promise that the mountains up high will lie at your feet. The rivers would part ways just so you can be carried on the backs of kings to a paradise unknown to men.
That every meal you taste will be ambrosia, the food of the gods and every mouthful will melt on your pallet perfectly to your organic delight.
I promise every thread that weaves the cloth for your clothes will be spun with a pure gold spindle and the material made will be interlaced together as lovers.
So that you are covered with fabric so perfect so soft so thin that your body is stimulated by your own movement.
I promise that your name will be spoken with pleasure. As if one was intimate with a lover of unspoken experience to unbearable satisfaction.
I promise that the milk for your bath will be pure, in a tub of gold, beaded with jewels. To be heated, by the breaths of a thousand virgins so that your skin is never tainted by unclean hands.
I promise that everything will be centered around you and everyone will bow down to your excellence. That everything you dream and everything that could be possible to imagine will be within your reach.
I promise that every word I speak to you now will be engraved in a book as if you were a god, to be worshiped for all eternity.

I promise!
I promise!
I promise!
And all these things I give to you, the only thing you required was my heart and that will eternally be yours. This I can promise!

Great

I speak for great. Great men and women who have built this world on their backs. Who have died in vain and can no longer speak for themselves.
I speak of great. Great moments in time that design the world frame into what we see now. Moments we no longer care to remember.
I speak to great. Great children that one day will seek knowledge of a world that has changed beyond recognition. This is the reminder that the past is now the future. Every moment we take will repeat itself because the world goes around in circles.
Speak of great, speak to great, feel greatness.
Greater that is in he that is in the world. Walk among great. The ultimate power is living for great, great minds, great hearts, and a great love.

Forward

I turn from you. I walk away with third degree burns and bleeding organs. I step on the scale and the weight of hurt was only relieved by the loss of me. Pulling the dead burden by my soul I move onward.
Forward

Lover he is not but with time I shall cure my flesh of its master. The ringing of voices keeps me in a daze, stop it! The road of gold leads to self-destruction.
Forward
The more I begin to be someone else planting seeds to harvest, the longer it takes to construct me after one drop of rain in a drought. I will still advance.
Forward
I am condemned to past mistakes because time travel has yet to exist. Now I no longer see your face with pleasure blinded by my sexual hunger.
Forward
I no longer talk of you with sugar, nor salt. I dare not even think of you. I pretend to be deaf to your name. I will get over you.
Forward
You cannot keep me on my self-made island of desertion I am free finding relief throughout love's endless experience. Headlong into a place of great pain I endure. Until I move to a place where you no longer exist by moving forward.

Some Things

Something old something new something borrowed something blue. Now as things fall into place on your perfect day. The day that is set among the cosmic stars as yours and the man who is destined to be your husband. You look at me. You ask in a nervous voice for advice on life. I turn you around so that you don't see my face or the tears in my eyes. Then I place your something borrowed around your neck. The pearls were elegant and beautiful shining with a perfect blend of tinted pink and blue. Each one not the same and yet each one defined to create one perfect piece. Then I stated I cannot tell you words of wisdom. The

start of every journey may take the same road but each traveler will see thing differently. So I tell you about the pearls. I say the pearls that you wear symbolize a marriage. That these pearls, which are so striking, hold the answer you wish to discover.
That each pearl has endless promises that you must take as one, promises of life, love, and happiness.
The circle of thread that connects you two together encrusting each one is the love that will hold you through all your day as man and wife.
That the gold clasp in the back, that locks together the row of pearls, is trust and commitment, the safeguard of every marriage.
And that the color means every day can bring a mixture of both happiness and sadness. Nevertheless with the love that you share the sadness will always end with a smile.
Then you turn around and smile at me. You say to me that the pearls will always be a treasure to your heart. That the pearls themselves were not the something borrowed that you had been waiting for but the words were.
And you hope to one day place them around my neck when my time comes.

Spare Me

Spare me all your lies and confusion. All your promise and disillusion.
All your words of love. All your prayers up above.
All the thing you said you would do. All the little things, the big things and everything in between too.
All the You that wasn't brand new. All the time when I was feeling blue.
All your friends who covered it up. All your family that was corrupt.

All the girls that took my place. Even the ones that dare to get in my face.
Spare me
All pictures of us together. And the family that you wanted for forever.
All the hotels where you were caught. All my dreams of man and wife that's not.
All the beautiful moments in time. Every child born to you that wasn't mine.
All the good days the bad days and the starting over.
Everyone I used to cry on their shoulder.
All things that I purchased and you bought. All the reasons why and days that we fought.
The car, the house, and all our stuff. Every moment we shared because I've had enough.
Spare me
All the moments that I was down. All the hurt pound for pound.
All the reason I left you for the same excuse. All the things I got over when I cut you lose.
All the periods I took you back. All the confidence that I had lacked.
All those problems is now of the past. I got me back so you can kiss my ass.
Even after all of that you assume that it would stay forever you and me. The one you were with me will never be.
Every second I look up above thankful I'm free. So for all the things you want to say spare me.

Why vs. How

A critical question for living, loving, and surviving life.
I ask myself why all the time.
I don't know his reasons, I wish I did.

I wish I could say that the day he walked away his heart was broken.
And that he sacrificed his happiness because he wanted me to have perfection.
That he cried a river because the pain was so great, it was as if they were physical blows not emotional.
I wish I knew what he wanted me to do with the agony.
My life wondering why.
Why he cheated?
Why he lied?
Why he left?
Why he said he loved me?
Why he couldn't love me?
Why am I so hurt?
Why the pain hasn't gone away?
Why I still think about him almost every day?
Why I wish I did thing differently?
Why?
I build this world in my head of why. And this world of why keep me confused. My mistake of course was that why didn't let me see the true essence of me. The woman who did everything he asked. The woman who took care of her man. The woman who could always make him smile. I started wondering where was this woman, this woman was dynamic she could paint a world of beauty on pictures of destruction. She could make a home on the foundation of fifteen cents. She could love and forgive within the same breath. With the woman I describe I had asked myself how.
How could he cheat on you?
How could he lie to you?
How could he leave you?
How come he said he loved you?
How come he couldn't love you?
How come you're still hurt?
How come the pain hasn't gone away?
How come you still think of him every day?

How could you have done thing differently?
How?
You see the difference between why and how was major. Why leaves me confused but how gives me my answers. How meant that I'm a strong woman who understands her value. As opposed to the why where he gives me my worth. Why was about him and how was about believing in me. Many women sit around wondering why when they should be focused on the how. How to be strong. How to move on. How to build a world with having no answer to why but by knowing the how. How to overcome it all. This one word is like the jack of its trades, with this world built on the hows, and not on the whys. This was something in itself, living for how. How the next man will fall in love with me. How I'm going make sure we smile. How the woman that I am will define us both. How why will never again be the focus of my lifestyle. The how without the why.

The Words for Sin

I tried to remember a time when I didn't want it. A period when I didn't look for. A moment when I wouldn't need it. The rush I got when I received it. Rocking the core of my flesh with the blissful pleasures of sin. Pastors peach about it, priests condemn for it, every religion across the board would tell you, that you can live without it. So why do it? Sin is simply doing something that is morally wrong. The rush the pleasure the passion to feel the forbidden. Life seem to kill for the desires to sin. Well my sin is simply the pen I hold in my hand. Rolling a surface of ink entering the center of my living body to thrust words of nutriment to a world that supports starvation. Words the pleasures of my heart giving a blast of heat that explored all over me. Bring me to my knees with delightful simulations of feeling. It not the pen or the words that are the sin but the power it holds over me. My will for something else collapsed crushing any dream to do anything other than put ink to paper. This sin is not great to many but there are others that suffer for this fixation. Other that every waking minute is stimulated with words that go beyond the normal. It gives me even more that a lover can give to dash off in secret and feel a poetic orgasm. Creating and giving birth to infamous thoughts a sin that will forever be my damnation.

My Word

My words, I thought had to be ocean deep,
Surrounding plates of land, hiding old and new treasures
I wanted to write the world an art piece, and beat notes of life on paper.
I thought…

I wanted to be loquacious with millions of nouns and verbs to out-word anyone
To drop brilliance in each line,
To choreograph thoughts to silent movement,
I thought…

I wanted to put words together in a chain of gold set to empower, shining with perfection.
To have them value as antique and place in the vault of the mind.
I thought…

My words, I thought were pieces of me displayed in museums, framed in an elegant language, portraits of masters.
I thought…

My words, I thought could free the simplest of minds and dazzle geniuses in the making, with a formation of worlds. I thought…

My words I realize would be talk about negatively, positively, and sometime not at all.

My words I knew would release their energy in clouds of blissful freedom.

Whether my words do anything else it doesn't matter.

My words will forever reflect the essence of me.

The Memo

I thought about this while I was sitting with a friend and she explained to me why she was taking her man back for the umpteenth time.
What can I say to her, do I say "again didn't he cheat on you." Which I knew would spiral our friendship to an end. Or "girl I'm so happy for you." Then I would be subconsciously hating me for fooling myself about the continuation of this relationship. I could talk about God. Give her that old scripture on how the Father can create miracles. That speech always brings about false hope. Then eventually when they break up she would just blame me and God.
But in reality my mind wasn't even paying attention to her. All I can think about was "didn't she get the memo."
The memo being that this relationship was not going to work. Not why she's the only one changing. Not her lifestyle but her mind. Not her goals but her dreams. The

only thing in this relationship she cared about was getting to an altar. I wanted to explain the church house is always open for the altar. "She must not have got the memo."
I wanted say "Girl he's not going to change until he wants it." I believe you can bring a horse to water but until he's ready he's not going to drink. She's a woman carrying a man who has little faith and not enough strength to change. Who has all the answers but couldn't understand that reality was the questions. Who doesn't have the ability to pray to a higher being. "He must not have got the memo." So what do I do? Nod my head in ways that may or may not be an agreement. Smile and say nothing so she wonders if I'm for or against their relationship. As a friend do I keep hope alive? "They couldn't have gotten the memo."
The memo about living life. That happiness comes from within. NO matter how hard you try to be with someone if that person is not trying then the relationship is fail before it begins. The memo that states we grow and learn with everything we do. That everyone should embrace change because it's inevitable. That love once found will break all barriers. And if its truth love, love can give everlasting happiness. "Did they really not get the memo?"
This memo was up everywhere how come they didn't get it. As I continue to think to myself I realize that she has gone silent and was looking at my face with tears in her eyes.
And when I ask what was wrong, she stated "Yes I got the memo but I couldn't understand it."

I Am

Tell me what you see
Because honey you sure don't see me

I am the queen of ebony a glistening pearl like the black opal
For my style my attitude everything that's me sure ain't for sale
I carry myself as if I were made of the finest silk
But you tried to crush me like roses that were already wilt
You criticize me because I'm a proud black woman of color
But that ain't fair just look in the mirror brother
Yes I want a man with things of his own
But it takes a virtuous woman to make a house a home
You say you do everything I do nothing but complain
When I carried you like God in the sand please explain
How are you walking, because I am your backbone.
You may think you wear the crown but I am the power behind the throne
"Oh you don't need me" you said as if you rule the world
But the King of Soul said it best it nothing with a woman or a girl
My life is a breeze you say, you think it easy walking in my shoes.
From the time I wake up to the time I lay down this hard-working black woman you will lose
You won't do black because a black woman is a gold digger
My mommy say if a man don't want to work sit on his behind then he must be a.......
Yo man black son the white man got you down
No wig no nose no make-up in sight and still you look like a clown
Oh I'm leaving I'm going to find a real man so it's time I say goodbye
But let me tell you this I am a woman a black woman am I.

I'm Selling Myself

What is the value of self-worth? What is the cost for the physical body of a person? What would you price a human being at?
What 20 dollars? No maybe 200 or even 2000? How would I price myself? After all it's not a new market Negro-selling just ended somewhat one or two centuries ago. Oh and I can't use the woman slavery thing because women are still being sold in some third world country. Now that I think about it I guess it is something OF A NEW CONCEPT. After all I'm the one selling me. Not for sex no, or for work definitely not nor for mutilation I love myself. No I'm just selling me past me future me and all me in between. I really have no idea what I'm doing or how to go about selling me.
I just know there are physical things in this world that I need. Food clothes a car a house six-thousand-dollar jeans. I also think to myself that after I get the money for me will I be able to spend it on me.
Then again what do I do about advertising myself? Do I list all my good qualities or do I just describe myself. Do I tell about the things that I can do or do I list the things I love to do?
I do want the best price after all you can only sell yourself once in your lifetime and then there's nothing left to sell.
I just really need to figure this out. The market of self-selling is a broad and open market because some people mistakenly sell themselves. They don't know that the money value that they put on themselves is worthless. And that the mind body and soul are precious unto God so it is priceless. Just think about this all the people who sell themselves some rappers politician actor doctor etc... It is said that everyone has a price? I'm just advertising mine... But ask yourself what's your price?

And I can't get mad at myself because it was me that sold me.
And what more I can't feel sorry for myself because I got me into this.
I just came up with this plan and I thought to myself why not sell yourself. You can get a good price for yourself.
So I'm selling myself I'm pretty sure that me and myself is worth it.

Pity Party

I'm throwing myself a pity party.
Not to be mistaken for a petty party that's what he's throwing.
No, no I need people to feel my loss….. Because I don't.
Yes ladies I am in need of every drop of tenderness. I want all your sympathy. Shaking your heads as you give sad looks of sorrow. And please don't forget misplace words of compassion.
I need everyone to remind me that he'll regret everything he did. All his cheating, his lying, and his ugliness.
And that he'll never find another woman better than me.
Because really I could care... less of everything he thinks, says, and does, for now on that is some other suck... I mean woman's problem.
In my tears I realize something that he'll never change.
Looking back to all those selfish things he did that I thought were cute but were really just that selfish. All those moments I was making excuses for his action that were just that… his actions.
Oh don't get me wrong when he decided to walk out on me I cried I even asked God why?
I thought I was to blame I had driven him away.

And then I came to appreciate that I'm too good of a woman for him.
And he could not come up to part with his big ego.
In reality I'll be his true regret, hopefully he'll find someone else to fill the hole in his chest.
While I'm living in my world of self-contain, I know he's in a world with heartache and pain.
You know he did me a favor so I have secretly moved on. I'm throwing this party someone can tell him I've held strong.
And when people say I'm destroyed and depressed I want him think that now he has the best. I don't want that nigger at my door please. It's not about who ended it first it's about my self-worth.
I'm thinking this will ultimately catch on. Ladies it's time to throw yourself a pity party hell you'll never go wrong.

Hurt

The lost world of reality appears before my eyes. I am hurt the burning breath in my stomach gives no relief to my pain. If I would have… but I could have… Regret becomes common thought hunting my imagination with more superior results. Words fail to come to me as my hourglass turns into a desert drowning the foolish.
Faint please black out I whisper to be still for all moment in time.
While air keeps leaving my lungs with no replacement for more I see red. Hurt I keeping thinking why, why, questioning every god over a multitude of religions. The suffering keeps me drugs leaving me not connecting to any one gods'… I try to pray but words cannot link through the cell of black mist that is life. No promise of relief can bring peace to a lost soul. Hurt help as the casket of confusion

buries me in the bleeding of life. The scream of another life continues to cut deeply across my flesh. The amputation of all my limbs would still not surpass the distress of sorrow. The simple word of pain does not begin to contain what I would describe as the penetration of a million swords inserted into one mind. Hurt tears of affliction scorch over my face compounding the stampede of a thousand days of self-inflicted pain. The only description of what I am feeling would be to go over a mountain cliff and live paralyzed with the pain. To have millions of insects eating your flesh while lying in hot coals. Hurt the misery of living life with no death in sign for your corpse. The word for pain becomes so little when confronted with a pain so great the world has yet to define. Hurt.

I Love That Nigger

I am in love with a sorry ass nigger. Nigger is a word that I had previously refused to use when describing the love of my past life. Oh I tried saying tired but tired did not define the man of my nightmare once upon my dreams. Oh yeah I tried using immature but growing up was a male thing which would apply to all men. I wanted to use flash-words to describe this nigger, words in motion to define my nigger but that nigger could only be labeled by one word. He was a nigger.
I wish I could say Negro so his ignorant ass could move with the struggle of black power. Or African American to say our root was deeply rooted by a path of heroic colored people. I wanted to take out color all together and just define him as my mate.
Oh but that nigger had a problem. He was mixture of stupid, and black with a tablespoon of arrogant. Two

teaspoons of education one pound of country. Two whole
cups full of shit put on 360 degrees to make a nigger.
What is this how did I miss this nigger I thought I would
spot a nigger even in my sleep?
And what am I supposed to do with this nigger? Believe me
I tried everything.
How would I live my life with loving a nigger?
I keep thinking that maybe it's not love but he do
something nigger-like and I'm in love all over again.
Making excuses on why he may be a nigger I promise you
this is love. I'm sure if you're a nigger-lover you probably
doing the same thing. So I'm proud to say that I'm in love
with a sorry ass nigger.

The Essence of Kay

She a mystery unto herself.
Educated and validated on the road to wealth.
Honey girl is a movement of style.
Although the world may not yet see she a high profile.
Her class is in her DNA.
A born queen elegant imbedded in her sway.
What she lack in character she make up in confidence.
Straight up and down paper chaser she ain't worried about
no cents.
Oh this girl is jazzy mixed with the deep sound of blues.
Dazzling classic, twisted rock, and opera-infused.
No brick house here honey that girl a stunning hour glass.
Maintaining her classy flair despite the fact time has pass.
She a real woman cowards need not apply,
If sister girl what you want honey you better learn how to
fly.
Speaking lightly is not her thing so please pay attention.

African deep, worlds of the unknown, heck this girl is from another dimension.
Oh you may try but sugar you can't never keep her down
She got to be a descendant of Muhammad heavyweight pound for pound.
Sister girl a warrior she a lioness in the jungle of life.
Yes she maybe is single now but she even more powerful as a wife.
There different levels to this lady you can't ever understand.
She has built and destroyed worlds with a pen stroke in her hand.
I think you comprehend the dynamic Katenna a little today
You better believe this is just a short intro to the essence of Kay.

You Don't Know

You think just because you hear it that it has to be true. Oh I hear a lot of things that even worse than that about you.
You think just because you wrote it that everyone will believe. That no one will question the writer you couldn't conceive.
You think just because you read it that it has to be the gospel in full. Its smelling stink, full of shit but you don't think it bull.
You don't know me.
You don't know my mind and the worlds I create. You just see success so on that you got to hate.
You don't know what keep me here or how I started. You just see how high I am and that you and I have parted.
You don't know my life or the person I've become. You just see the dollar signs and think I owe you some.
You don't know me

So why is it that now all my old friends finally remember my name. Everyone sending me free stuff to get closer to the game.
So why is it that now all my old male associates all got me in bed. If everyone of them paid a dollar a whole country would be fed.
So why is it that now I have more relatives then I can ever remember. It like everyone want to join team Kay and become a member.
You don't know me
I sit back and laugh about all the negativity that come my way. Even knowing that my God carry me from day to day.
So this is a shout out to everyone who does this to someone else. Instead of using faith, consistency, and hard work for themselves.
So now you know that in reality to me you don't exist. So keep doing you because you don't know me that you couldn't miss.

Him

The sweet sound of music plays inside my head when he speaking in a room surrounded by tens, or even thousands. I watch the vocal motion of a man who I've placed above all men. The discovery of Him a religion to worship the core of this one man. I'm falling deeper into his principles trying to remind myself that he is someone else's. Then the fantasy of him and I becomes reality to my mind. I dream of moments where his words graze my shoulder and trace my neck. Moments where pleasure is won in a second but is imprinted on my feelings for a lifespan. The destruction of his world would be agony to my living soul. It is him that I want not his life just the man for days, hours, minutes, and seconds just so he can answer the call of my

praises. The touch of faith that will enable he and I to breathe the same air. Outtake for him intake for me.
Him the man I form a literature liaison in a world that doesn't exist. The pleasure of my mind in being near him keeps me praising this full god. Am I in love with him; no this is Him not to love but to obsess over his thoughts. To wander into the poetic melody of his words and play the rhythm in the tone in sync to my heart. The creator of words that has released passion in my mind. Burned holes into the fabric of society dreams to a world of unknown.
Him

That

I loved that…
I loved that he give me space even when he hold me close.
I loved that whenever I tell him something he write it down so he can read it later.
I loved that he can't remember by birthday but never forget the day we met.
I loved that I'm forgetful with my phone but he always find a way to reach me.
I loved that when I'm not perfect he still wants me at his side.
I loved that my wants are his personal needs.
I loved that he has to hear my voice just to close his eyes at night.
I loved that if I don't finish what I started he will try to finish it for me.
I loved that he loves me before and after I change me again.
I loved that he may not get my happy endings but with him I'm happy.
I loved that when I'm mad he make me laugh.

I loved that he a man but still act like a boy when I'm being immature.
I loved that when he's around the smile linger on my face. That he sweet to my crazy family. That he doesn't complain when I late. That he think I'm silly. That he seem to want me forever. That I can talk to him in the middle of the night knowing he has to go to work 5 o'clock in the morning. That his dreams are mostly of me and him. That he believe we have a future. And he see me as his princess even with my hair standing up on my head. And he thinks I'm sexy wearing his boxers.
That what I want to be in life doesn't matter as long as I'm being it with him.
I loved that he late for work because he couldn't stand leaving the bed with me it.
I loved that the smile on his face is the first thing I see when he look at me.
That even when I'm not all me he still feel the need to be there. I loved that he love me. That he knows I'm in love with him. And that most of all that there's something in me worth loving.

Time

Where did it go? Where is it now?
I thought I had it in the palms of my hands. You see before I started this journey I had plans, I said to myself that this is where I want to be. That I will continue on forward. Now this where I still am at the beginning where I started. Looking back I was still thinking I had it. That I could do this that I will do this. Don't worry I told myself I know what I'm doing. And now I've lost it. Lost in the movement of my conscious mind. It's funny when I look around me at others they seem to have it in spades. Where is it? I tried to

find it even though I know it will never truly be mine. The waiting, the wanting, the thinking I have plenty. So where did it go how come I didn't see it? How come it won't stop for me? Why didn't I feel it until it was gone? Why am I still waiting for it? You see it in the planning, too much thought in anything means nothing will ever get done. Simply the airplane will never stop I will have to jump off with or without a parachute. That's so I can land on my feet. But I finally figure it out I'm too scared to even get on the plane. So what do I do now wait it out, pretend I still have it, while I know it's gone. Do I at this point ask for help? If I ever want to get where I'm going maybe I should just ask someone for help. The fear will never let me do anything without planning. So as I continue to plan how to plan to ask for help. I realize more and more that it is moving further and further away. Finally I stop at this I give up because I'm all out of... time.

My Mr. Gray

In one moment, this one man changed my life my dear Mr. Gray.

The history of me can be explained by my relationships with these men Mr. Black, Mr. White, and my Mr. Gray. Only one has conquered my heart in ways that have left me in a balance of serenity. Conveying their story is a characterization that defines me.

Mr. Black
He was my nightmare the reincarnation of this man kept appearing in my life when things were always unstable. This man Mr. Black seemed to want me to do and say things that were not like me.

The spell of destruction and carelessness was his life style. I believed his lies so easily falling prey to his words of beauty. Mr. Black. Black was his mind, black was his heart and black was his testimony. Just a grave of skeletons in one plot. I knew then to live with this men would make me a black widow spider living for her next prey. Only taking never understanding why always alone.

Mr. White
He was the dream of an actual mind in perfection appearing when things were morally high. Mr. White seemed to focus on what is traditional forgotten instead of today's society. That things were in a state of confusion and disillusion wanting me to believe that this was the only road to bliss. Cleaning everything in painted white solid blank no start no finish one color one believe. White washing everything, t's with no crosses i's with no dots. Mr. White. White intelligent white affection and white was his damnation. Just a perfect blend of white on the wall. Living for white was a driving force to insanity that would leave me a cuckoo bird dropping eggs in other nest. Never staying to listen always walking away.

My Mr. Gray
Now he was my reality in a dream with no perfections. The force of his being was supreme when he appeared life and action seemed to become one. Bringing focus and strength in a twisted entity of matter. He was never wrong or right just the discovery of balance in one alliance. The world power of understated events and overinflated judgments laid dormant at my feet. My Mr. Gray was a living movement sweeping across nations with compassion and mercy. Questions and answers coming together in a marital bliss. Mr. Gray had wisdom, knowledge, and understanding. He was overflowing with love so I accepted him in my heart. He believed the world was a treasure to be

discovered. Opening my eyes to a rainbow-colored world reds, greens, blues, yellows, and more. After meeting him no one else could compete, he made everything that Mr. Black or Mr. White was look gloomy and bleached. He made me feel like I was a fairy with magical wings with the belief that anything could happen. With everything being possible always beginning afresh.

Mr. Gray also made me realize that every color could be changed into another. Meeting him put life in its place and me facing the world with my own paintbrush.

The Lady

"Ain't nothing fancy about a base born whore," she said but I recognize I was different. We were all women of the world. Posing with cater goods for any tasty gentleman's needs. How I performed to entertain them was different. I made them believe the love, that I would do anything to fulfill the pleasures of flesh. She was just another angry whore who had spread her legs one too many times. I was a showcase slowing building a throne and looking down from the seat. The pleasure of one man after another was never for me. They got furious when I would only entice one, dwelling on the confused state of my reality. Buying my time with ill-gotten gains but the lifestyle was never for me. I was a sweet girl child, who turned into a beautiful female teen that led to an angry sophisticated women. Family wherever they are may God rest their souls. My anger made me fight but I did it with a smile. The imprisonment of supporting what's mine with their blood money. My blood intoxicating the river for this alcohol-induced existence. I am her the child within the woman who had gone through life on bended knee. Crying for toys of my past 'cause the woman has as of yet not been discovered. No one hears my cry but me. I perform never missing a beat to whatever tones that's me. You know looking back I knew they wouldn't understand me. The whores of the street because that was who they were. I myself was a lady.

Her

Her first smile,
Her first frown,
Her first laugh,
Her first tear,
Her first accomplishment,
Her first failure,
The moment to protect the first the race to cover her in shields. Her the child her the teen her the woman her your love. She is I, not The I in me but the rebel of ignorance. The one that stakes her claim on the heart with an ice pick in the chest. She and I were destined to be born female within the world of men. Our first steps are parallel to every milestone we pass. Never taken together but either way taken none the same. The first time you notice her smile doesn't meet her eyes. The display of false happiness blinds the truth of pain. She and I The She within the I. My first, her first, repeating lost memories of good times in your mind. The time of innocence has fallen away to leave the mature woman with the heart of a child. She is truly the female within the cat landing on all fours. The place in you that is guarded with every breath because she is me The Me within thee.

Super Hero

I find myself in a job I didn't ask for or even want. Please don't talk about how the economy is down or that at least I have a job. That's something I already know I just wish that my job came with vacation time, no on-call 24/7, a lunch break and even a paycheck. All those hassles but the only thing this job comes with is extreme powers and unlimited strength. What's my job you ask, I'll tell you. I'm a super hero. I know its crazy right. I have to pretend I'm extremely strong, and fight off bad guys. Being a super hero is no joke, it not the same as a hero. Anyone can be a hero but I'm a super hero. Super like Spiderman, Batman, and Superman of course and the list can go on for super heroes. Although come to think about it there's not that many women in my field. I wonder why that is. Anyway the worst part of my job is I can't hide my identity like the other super heroes. Hell sometimes I want to go where no-one knows my name. I can't because the pedestrians: kids, family, exes, and friends would find me. But do you know what? Funny they don't even know which super hero I am. Hell I get mistaken for Wonder Woman or Superwoman all the time. They think I spin around and magically appear in a star-spangled banner bathing suit. Or maybe I dash into a phone booth and come out in a cheerleading outfit with a cape. Not to put down my co-workers but I'm a different breed altogether of woman super hero. Plus I don't even have a cool super hero name. In many different languages I am called maid but I call myself mother. You see my strength lies in my ability to change myself and personality at the speed of light. I'll explain I have to be mom, friend, peacemaker, sister, etc. all at the same time and at a moment's notice. As if that wasn't hard enough I have to have the ability to clone myself to make a lot of me so that I will be able to save everyone as needed. I know what you're thinking you think a lot of women do that but I have to do it with a smile. What you missed your bus? I'll be there. What your man left you again? No no I'm on my way. What your car got stolen? This super hero is here to save the day. Don't say it, it's not easy being me in fact who's going to save me when I need saving. I guess I have to I'm a super hero right. I really need to find another job.

Ebony Queen

Mixing reminiscences of females long forgotten with a soul that can break through generations. Using knowledge that walks in the shadows of light faced with ignorant. Within this woman embracing enormous obstacles is the making of a queen. Holding firm to her past she walks among royalty with her head held high. Breaking the backs of ancestors to rise above her grief and pain. Not born to lead but born to impact the lives in the world surrounding her. Justice is just a word of the misguided which has placed her in a situation that's bottomless. Claiming her rights to rule a multicolor nation she is queen. Many will follow the lady's place on the throne with willpower and drive. Although there are others determined to pull don't this woman with the purest of heart. She carries the embodiment of African legends in the rod of her back. She is implanted with the wisdom of past queens and kings in her bloodline. This woman that gives life to the lost souls of ancient tribes with the purpose that we will overcome. I would like to say I am she the queen that defies history that she is me a woman that has yet to be known. This woman this ebony queen is one that is known to many ask anyone and they will tell you. All I have to say is that her name is defined as fawn a young deer in Hebrew. Giving that words have synonyms and full circle is how the father brings us here is another meaning for her name; be obsequious to, be sycophantic to, curry favor with, crawl to, and ingratiate oneself with. She is a reason for change and that is what makes her an Ebony Queen.

My Rose (LTJ)

The words of life's foundation placed in my heart by a rose. Layered soft, beauty skin deep, and thorns undiscovered. My rose was aging in the sun over my lifetime. The deep red passion in her was my living blood. The goddess blooming in the blossom of men. In the loss of time she shed her petals abandoning the garden her energy released to mist. I sacrifice her to my heart. Living with the memories of words spoken but not taken. I see her dancing in the sun by the wind forever my rose. Never wilting, sweet smelling, a touch of beauty. My rose.

Sister of Me

The sunlight of perfection shines on me as I look on you. Although we are not blood the bonds of our souls has infused though the painful struggle of simply being women. Together we carry the broken pieces of our heart collected with the puzzles of our life mistakes. Now as we begin to travel the road of recovery we see each other. Life's desert of destruction has left both of us hungry and dehydrated for a companion. Our walk in the sand has led to us to the same oasis of relief. While you offer the water of friendship to cleanse the hurt and pain. I offer bread of love to soothe the mistrust and confusion. During moments of our laughter and love I return to me. I pray in those moments you return to you. A you that is stronger to carry yourself in the sand with God when we are separated. Those moments when I am not there to comfort you, and the times when you cannot reach me. Our love for each other has made us queens of our destiny. Looking on the world with an abundance of faith treasure in our heart. I recognize the thread of love that connects us together I called you by heart sister of me.

Mother Love

Driven she tries another bill in the mail but she's not surprised. She smiles with no regrets with eight kids to support what did you expect? She is a mother, to have four sisters and me, plus three brothers. She made home the neighborhood, having two jobs, cooking and cleaning doing the best she could. Working eighteen-hour days making ends meet, taking care of all of us to her was no major feat. We would stay up just to see her face, even when she was tired her present was simply grace. She is a lady that held her own even with so much on her plate she didn't complain or mourn. Mama is a spiritual woman like many, believing God was the answer so when the blessings came they were plenty. Visits to the park with no worries in sight she would pray for hours while all of us were sleeping at night. She must have done something because we all turned out right, I'm still happy to see her smile shining bright. Everyone's grown but we still look back realize now although she would do without there was nothing we lacked. She's still saying seek God up above even with the eight of us I always felt my mother's love.

Irrational

I'm crazy.
I having delusions of you and it's confusing to me.
I can't stop the replaying of moment of me riding the wave of lust.
For playing in heat a melting liquid of motion. Back-to-back thoughts of us.
Slowly making me insane, you're all I think about talk about.
Fantasies have me in a loop of dreams leave me in bliss.
You said I would come back when I left. Debating my mind with my soul. Hell now I'm talking to myself, and she winning.
The control over my body of my world is damaging to my heart.
It been six months, three hours, four minutes, 19, 20, 21 seconds since our last moments together but who's counting. I wish I didn't know that.
Not that you would know but I left my ears to the floor and I figure she's taken care of all your needs.
Memories illusions of looks on your face when I did something she just wouldn't do. Something your mind couldn't take in at night in the dark.
Daylight has you in a sweat harvesting control.
What have I done to be tormented by my lips on your neck my nails in your back the scent of your hunger.
Why is that now the feeling of butterflies wanting you to storm the gate of my levee and conquering the very being I was losing?
I can't stand you. Yes I know how this sounds but I'm crazy. Why else do I fight with myself in a battle that is destined to hurt?
The feel of my hands' replica of yours is an instant joy of emptiness. The chase to come and feel complete.

No, to feel whole. Complete could only leave me finished.
Whole gives me all the right pieces.
As if nature agrees to this union.
It's just that I am a perfect example of a mental case for psychological study. Running with that I mimic others to pass under the radar.
Is this normal when my world is not you. That I can still breathe on earth is amazing. Maybe it is but I'll just keep this to myself and continue to argue one day soon I hope to win.

(I Am) The She in Me

I am the theft you caught me stealing away every drop of blood. Bleeding you dry until your skeleton fell at my feet. I am the bitch, slut, whore, and every other simpleminded thing you can come up with, with your prepaid education and field slave knowledge. And dollar store logic that stated you're the best of all mankind. I am and can be everything you want me to be. I can say and act with the drama that all black women of my kind do. Giving time I can become that ignorant ass backyard stupid woman you say I am. Although time and time again you shared your words with anyone that would listen stepping on your high horse. The victim of your own selfishness the one who has given and continues to give. I am the taker the one with the hard heart leaving you dying with your self-inflicted wounds. I am the woman that broke you. The one that you can't stop thinking about even when you're fucking her. The one who gave you more than you deserve and took only what you offer. I am she who is all-powerful I will not bend I am not broken you can go around me and you can't go through me. I am me and even when you try I will never be beneath your feet. I am her the ultimate she and she is me. I am.

With These Words

Words the most powerful tools at hand. Commanding life and death with the speed of light. Penetrating the heart and piercing the soul. Shape swords cutting the organs to steads. Making the world clean washed anew seeing the light within the darkness. Words can continue to plant seeds that will harvest until the extinctions of mankind. It is the giver and taker, the love and hate, the hopelessness and faithfulness of perfect dreams and broken nightmares. Words, the poetic movement of life within the mind. It is within these words that my world was formed and that the foundation became solid. The words of believe and strength the words of discovery and power. Words, life tools for wisdom, knowledge, and understanding.

Letter to Myself

Dear Me,

When I put these words on this paper I wondered what it would say. What could I say to you in a letter that I could not tell you to our face? Then I realize that I needed to address this letter to someone else. Not the brain me or the heart you but she the soul. The child that is lost to the adult. When we became the woman we are now I thought we had everything. I was caught up in getting there and maturing like all the other girls. I did not recognize that she was afraid to go. All this time she was not there to take the journey with us, and you and I cross that road alone. Our life was happening so fast we didn't stop to breathe. Everything was coming at us love, hurt, responsibilities, I could not even take the time I need for me much less she. I cannot say when I comprehended that she was not there. I'm just sorry I left her when she needed us the most. You and I were doing what was needed and did not feel the loss. I guess she can say we were selfish with our decision without her. So now we are here where we need her the most.

Everything in life is coming full circle because now you and I are at the beginning once again. Without her we are back where we started. Even when we aged we still have not grown. I can tell her this, that although we have success it is nothing without faith. And we even have goals but they're useless without drive and determination. You and I keep arguing because we started questioning the decisions that each other's making. If she came back and we all took that step then we would be strong. I cannot make her come she has to do it when she's ready. All I can say is that until then all of us will never get where we are supposed to be. With this letter I'm writing to her at least she can now understand that we did not mean to leave her and sorry it take so long to come back for her. She has a lot to teach us plus she can tell she was missed and this time we'll all take the journey together no matter how long it take. Let her take her time. She will become stronger and you and I now know without her we're nothing.

Fallen (Wasted)

Don't look, but I have to?
Just do it but am I ready?
I want it I can see it I believe in it.

Can I jump for it?
Could I really do this?
At this moment I am ready. I am ready to dive in. It's calling and telling me that this is mine. This where I belong. That everything will happen and I will land once I take this step. I will be released. I want to so badly the blood rushing to my core I am an addict I'm wasted. This high that I am on keeps me on a level above myself. Please don't judge me because the weight of my stones does more than penetrate glass. I can stretch my hands in dreams pulling them close to reality. Making them move across the red into a sea of fulfillment. It's not saying you want it, it's the doing the fear of success. The fear of great, not the rock and the hard place. There is nothing but air no gear, no plane, no parachute, just the fall. What's stopping me why can't I move am I lost in space asleep? I'm wasted too scared to transform too hungry to turn back and too stupid to know the difference. I'm addicted to the planning of my fall then falling. What is on the side of this squared world? My logic tells me we can discover anything but the medication leaves me without reason. Do I sit here and carry the old folk telling of encounters that are mythical? The tree of life is forever repeating itself so do I wait for another lifespan? Possibly being reincarnated to do in two lives what I could do in the one that is here now. Some time I dream that I fell on top more by accident than on purpose. If I could run it would be so much easier to take the fall but I plan then turn away. The freedom to taste what you eat and accept the pleasure of food. I am ready to fall.

Passing By

The silent drama of the forgotten. The whispered wind of perished trees blowing in the storm. The pasting of life onto the wings of discovery. Dropping of tears in the ocean of breath. Listening for words unspoken, words overlooked, words of forgiveness. Time is no more to the past of life. A walk among the living to fall among the dead. They sing of memories of time spent. Failing to recall the moments of happiness. Living with no end to words misunderstood. To see now that love is an eternal gift and expressing them is a blessing to the living. Hearing them is a request from the death. And feeling them is the ultimate for living life.

A Broken Love Song

How I got over you, well that I don't know? One morning I woke up after endless tears and moments of fear. The fear of never having happiness. The fear of being alone. The fear of always loving you. The fear of loving someone that is not you. The fear of wanting you too much to think. Somehow it started fading to numbness. Dulled by the moments of waiting for time to pass. Waiting on hours to go by to heal. Days of thinking that it would never go away. Remembering us arguing and loving. Talking and living. Dreaming and believing. I love you with a selfish heart wanting to be everything you wanted me to be. Now I'm just me, not a part of you. In myself I made an asylum of padded walls of love. I guess you can say that it was me continuing to look at you that finally allowed the sun after the storm. Who am I to say that you didn't make the best decision when you left? Chipping away the dream of lovebirds forever lost was the woman with strength to carry on. Our love was like a drop of blood in the sea of life regrets. Washing away to nothing. I hope you're happy because I am now.
How I got over you, well that I don't know? Where I am I know that the feel of you was paradise. You can continue to

be the person you are but I have change. I will see the clouds up high and breathe once more. I am smiling as I sing you this because my life is now my own. But who am I to say when I got over you it wasn't the best thing for me.

The Love I Want

I want a forever kind of love.
A love to embrace but leave no mistakes.
The kind of love that gives chase but doesn't slap you in the face.
A love that leave room to grow.
This kind of love can be taken fast or move slow.
Not a love that takes too long or goes with the flow.
A love that's higher than a kite or gets down low.
A forever kind
A lot of fighting for real or just for play.
A serious love or light and gay
A love that leaves you with something to say.
The endless kind that makes your day.
The kind that always gives a little more.
A love that will go throw a window if you lock the door.
The love that's in the heart and spreads to the core.
A kind of love that can fix anything even when it tore.
That what I want
A love that makes you smile and that funny,
A lasting love between times broke with loans or rich with money.
A love that's sweet with the taste of honey
The kind that leaves gifts like the tooth fairy or Easter bunny.
Love with a curve or a twist,
A love you hold tight in the palm in a fist.
This kind of love that's forever ending with a kiss.

Love that hurts when miss.
That's the love I want.

Sold

The highest bidder will always win the booty.
I sit here wondering what has become of me now that I am at an age of wisdom.
What has bought me from moments of stupidity?
Why am I now living life to its fullest and chasing the dreams that are fading?
I am sold.
Sold I thought I was selling myself.
Reality is the key to life, when we hit gold and feel it in the palm of our hands.
My reality was that I was never my own.
How can you sell something that you don't own?
Isn't that illegal?
Though all the promoting and advertising, pricing and financing, planning and forecasting, I have nothing to sell.
Believe or not it was already sold.
I'm trying to figure this out.
It's sold when was this I don't remember signing any consent forms.
Hell I didn't even receive a check.
This isn't like a dream I will eventually wake up from.
It is legal, a lawyer has contacted me and everything,
saying that I will be sued if I continue to pursue the matter of selling myself.
He stated that my owner is angry and will take full legal measures against me.
I got cocky and told him bring. It's funny how we only see the trip of the iceberg.
Everything I was, was shut down in the blink of an eye.

I realize my owner doesn't sleep. He's always watching over his properties.
All those times I thought I needed this and wanted that then things appeared just like magic.
The moment where I was lonely and needed a friend my owner was there taking care of me.
He's been carrying my key from the moment I was delivered from my mother's womb.
And I never knew because he was giving me time to come to him.
To accept him in full before he takes possession of me.
He doesn't want to own me and I resent him.
He wants me to have free will.
More and more as I thought about it I realize I always knew that I didn't own myself.
I was being led by society and in the ways of the world. Wanting a materialistic life style.
I am finally where he wants me to be. I know this seems funny but I like being owned by him.
I don't have to worry about anything. He carries me all the time even in sand.
I'm never lonely and he loved giving me my heart's desire.
I guess I was a little concerned how he would treat me.
How he could put up with me after all the things I've done? He explained that forgiveness will never be a problem.
You see he loves me not because he owns me. He loves me because I came to him with all of me and accept him fully.
I thank him every day by doing what little he asked of me. I also realize something I am happy it was him that bought me. So selling me was really never in question because like I just explained to all of you I'm already sold.

Twin

Trying to get away from her, looking in the glass of confusion and she always there.
My twin the person who I never wish to see. I hate her, I'm not her, stop thinking when you see me you see her. No matter what I do she appear. Her face is imprinted on mine. It drive me crazy watching her on every surface. Every time I change me all I can see is her, laughing at me. Taunting me with her face looking to see me. The eyes of a soulless person I am not her. It's funny that I bear her physical appearance how I wish for a blade, to correct my features. To edit the part of her I see in my mind. To redo the best part of the both of us. Wanting to rub my face against the wall of purity. Purging myself of her so I could never be her again. How can I take that memory of her ever existing so there can be only one of us? Why don't everyone stop judging me by her past mistakes? Reminding of how she was how she acted how she destroy. She was nothing, I am something, anything when compared to her. The scream of my innermost thoughts wants me to slay her and sacrifice her to the gods of wisdom. It hurt when someone calls me by her name. Bringing me down to a level of incompetence I rise above every time I'm down. She will be a figment of my imagination I will live to only be me. Her past mistakes will soon or later be destroy. So stop looking at me with her in mind I am no longer that foolish.

Could I Kill

Disclaimer: A question was asked to me at an age of youth, and being of a mind of confusion I answered. This was my reasoning in a moment of passion anything can happen and this is that moment. Please remember you also were young once. Thank you.

I watch the snake crawl out of your eyes,
The icepick in your back was a surprise.
The poison in your food killed you slow,
Telling me you cared… Now that was low.
I cut off your ears because you never heard me out,
The bullet through your head came out your mouth.
Now as you lie on the side of me dreaming deep,
I wonder really could I kill you when you sleep.

Final Words

I hope you enjoyed the first of many books to come. The next book will be coming out later this year. You can keep up with me from my website www.skatenna.com with my Blog I. A.M. (In Air Moments). Also all my social media Twitter @skatennaceo and @sellingkatenna. Instagram @skatenna and my facebook page Selling Katenna. I thank each and everyone, who has supported me. Stay Blessed

www.ingramcontent.com/pod-product-compliance
Lightning Source LLC
LaVergne TN
LVHW041237080426
835508LV00011B/1256